CW00762664

LOUIS WAIN

Übersetzung ins deutsche:
Bernd Kunzelmann.

Traduction en français:
Nicholas Powell.

Tous droits de traduction et d'adaptation
réservés pour tous pays.

© 2000, Bibliothèque de l'Image
46 bis, passage Jouffroy - 75009 Paris.
Tél. 01 48 24 54 14 - Fax : 01 45 23 08 83

Edition in english: ISBN 2-909808-91-2
Deûtsche ausgabe: ISBN 2-909808-92-0
Édition en français : ISBN 2-909808-80-7

THE CATS of LOUIS WAIN

DIE KATZEN von LOUIS WAIN

LES CHATS de LOUIS WAIN

PATRICIA ALLDERIDGE

Bibliothèque de l'Image

LOUIS WAIN AND 'THE LOUIS WAIN CAT'

'He has made the cat his own. He invented a cat style, a cat society, a whole cat world. English cats that do not look and live like Louis Wain cats are ashamed of themselves'.

This was the opinion of the writer H.G. Wells, whose appeal on behalf of the cat's inventor, then ill and nearly destitute, was broadcast in August 1925. My grandmother would probably have agreed with him. From time to time she would look at my own 1940s childhood cat 'Smokey', a thoroughly English cat who was certainly not ashamed of herself, and remark 'she looks just like a Louis Wain cat'. Oddly enough it never occurred to me to wonder what kind of cat this might be, or how it acquired its name. To me a 'Louis Wain cat' was something which simply existed in its own right, like other household brand-names such as 'Bird's custard powder' or 'Colman's mustard'. Many years later I was to discover that this was indeed precisely the status which it had once occupied, in households throughout the country.

I also discovered, after studying the creature with some care, that neither Smokey nor any other feline could ever look *just* like a Louis Wain cat: but it was part of Wain's great achievement that no one who admires his work and/or loves cats (often one and the same), can ever quite bring themselves to believe this fact. A good political cartoonist can convince us that his subject really does look exactly like the ever-more-extreme caricatures which appear daily on our breakfast tables. Louis Wain was a very good cartoonist, and even included a few political cartoons amongst his prolific output. The fact that the protagonists are always depicted as cats does not prevent them from being easily recognisable as political figures of the day, including the young Winston Churchill. He always denied

LOUIS WAIN UND DIE «LOUIS-WAIN-KATZE»

«Er hat sich die Katze sein Eigen gemacht. Er hat einen Katzenstil erfunden, eine Katzengesell-schaft, eine ganze Katzenwelt: Englische Katzen, die nicht so aussehen und nicht so leben wie «Louis-Wain-Katzen», schämen sich.»

Dies war die Ansicht des Schriftstellers H.G. Wells, dessen Hilferuf für den damals kranken und quasi mittellosen Erfinder der Katze im August 1925 gesendet wurde. Meine Großmutter hätte ihm wohl zugestimmt. Als ich ein Kind war, pflegte sie von Zeit zu Zeit meine Katze Smokey, eine durch und durch englische Katze, die sich mit Si-cherheit nicht ihrer selbst schämte, zu betrachten und sagen: «Sie sieht genauso aus wie eine «Louis-Wain-Katze». Seltsamerweise kam es mir nie in den Sinn, mich zu fragen, was für eine Katze das sein mochte oder wie sie zu ihrem Namen gekommen sein mag. Für mich war eine «Louis-Wain-Katze» etwas, das seine Daseinsberechtigung schlicht daraus bezog, dass es da war, genauso wie andere Markennamen in einem Haushalt, um nur «Bird's Pudding Pulver» oder «Colman's Senf» zu nennen. Viele Jahre spä-ter sollte ich entdecken, dass in der Tat genau dies einst der Status war, den sie in den Häusern im gan-zen Land eingenommen hatte.

Nach sorgfältigem Studium dieser Kreatur ent-deckte ich auch, dass weder Smokey noch irgendeine andere Katze jemals *genauso* wie eine «Louis-Wain-Katze» aussehen kann. Denn es war gerade Teil Wains großer schöpferischer Leistung, dass niemand, der sein Werk bewundert und / oder Katzen liebt (was meist auf das Gleiche herauskommt) sich dazu dur-chringen kann, dies zu glauben. Ein guter Zeichner politischer Cartoons kann uns davon überzeugen, dass sein Objekt wirklich genauso aussieht wie die immer extremer werdenden Karikaturen, die wir tagtäglich auf unserem Frühstückstisch vorfinden. Louis Wain war ein bemerkenswerter Cartoonist, und in sei-nem sehr umfassenden Werk finden sich sogar einige

LE CHAT « LOUIS WAIN »

« Le chat, c'est lui. Il a créé un style de chat, une société de chats, tout un univers du chat. Les chats anglais dont l'apparence et le com-portement ne ressemblent pas aux chats de Louis Wain n'ont pas de quoi être fiers. »

Tel était l'avis de l'écrivain H.G. Wells lors-qu'en août 1925 il fit appel, dans un message radiodiffusé, à la générosité du public en faveur de « l'inventeur » du chat, alors malade et in-digent. Ma grand-mère aurait sans doute été d'accord. Quand j'étais petite fille, dans les an-nées 1940, elle regardait de temps en temps mon chat Smokey qui, cent pour cent anglais, était assez fier de lui et elle lançait : « C'est un vrai chat Louis Wain. » Aussi curieux que cela puisse paraître, je ne me suis jamais demandé ce que signifiait ce sobriquet, ni comment mon chat l'avait attrapé. Pour moi, un « chat Louis Wain » c'était quelque chose qui avait tout sim-plement son existence propre, comme n'im-porte quelle marque alimentaire familière, Banania par exemple. Bien des années plus tard, je devais me rendre compte que de très nom-breux foyers à travers le pays partageaient mon opinion.

Au terme d'une étude assez approfondie de l'animal en question, j'ai également compris que Smokey ou n'importe quel autre chat ne ressemblerait jamais parfaitement au chat Louis Wain. Cependant, le génie de Wain est tel que tout admirateur de son œuvre et amateur de chats (ce qui revient souvent au même) admet difficilement cette évidence. Un bon dessina-teur politique possède l'art de nous convaincre que son sujet ressemble vraiment aux carica-tures de plus en plus poussées publiées tous les jours dans la presse. L'œuvre abondante du très bon dessinateur qu'était Louis Wain compte d'ailleurs quelques caricatures de politiciens. Il

that he caricatured the cat itself, and this may be literally true: but he brought to its portrayal that same quality of sharp-eyed, obsessive observation, and the ability to reduce his subject to a few stylized details with a quick stroke of the pen or pencil, which can make a good caricature almost more convincing than a portrait.

The Louis Wain cat does indeed, in some respects, look more cat-like than the real thing, having been reduced to its essential characteristics – a wide chubby face with a V-shaped mouth, huge eyes, a pliant soft-toy body, and small round feet with stuck-on pads which are clearly not designed for holding things. Superimposed on this feline outline is the characteristic which makes it instantly recognisable as a 'Louis Wain cat': its human expression, clothes, and actions. The fact that the cat itself retains its own feline identity even when appearing at its most human, is a measure of Wain's complete mastery of his subject. As a reviewer of one of his exhibitions wrote in *The Times*: 'It is not so much that he imparts human characteristics to the cat, as that he shows how cats would behave in human situations, and he does it with such sympathetic understanding of the essential cat, and such tact and economy of means, that we believe him.'

Over a period of more than thirty years, from the late nineteenth to the early- twentieth century, the Louis Wain cat established itself as a familiar sub-species of *felis domesticus*, entertaining children and adults alike, and subtly altering attitudes to its real-life progenitor, the domestic cat itself. The affection in which it was held contributed lasting benefits to animal welfare in general, and the welfare of cats in particular. It brought amusement and delight to many thousands of people, and continues to do so to this day. Its author's name became a household word, recognised and loved throughout

politische Cartoons. Die Tatsache, dass die Helden immer als Katzen abgebildet sind, hindert uns jedoch nicht daran, sie leicht als politische Figuren ihrer Zeit wiederzuerkennen - unter ihnen auch den jungen Winston Churchill. Wain hat stets bestritten, dass er die Katze selbst karikiere. Streng genommen mag das stimmen, jedoch brachte er in seine Darstellungskunst eben genau jene Qualität der scharfsichtigen, obsessiven Betrachtung und die Fähigkeit, sein Sujet mit einem schnellen Feder- oder Bleistiftstrich auf ein paar stilisierte Details zu reduzieren, die eine gute Karikatur fast überzeugender machen können als ein Porträt.

Tatsächlich sieht die «Louis-Wain-Katze» nach ihrer Reduzierung auf die grundlegenden Charakteristika in mancher Hinsicht mehr wie eine Katze aus als ihr Original: ein breites, pausbäckiges Gesicht mit V-förmigem Mund, riesige Augen, ein einem Plüschtier gleichender elastischer Körper und kleine, runde Pfoten mit aufgesetzten Ballen, die eindeutig nicht dazu geschaffen sind, etwas zu halten. Diese Skizze einer Kätzin wird überlagert von den Eigenschaften, die sie sofort als eine «Louis-Wain-Katze» erkennbar machen: ihr menschlicher Ausdruck, ihre Kleidung und ihre Art zu agieren. Die Tatsache, dass die Katze ihre eigene kätzische Identität beibehält selbst wenn sie auch noch so menschlich erscheint, lässt Wains vollständige Beherrschung des ursprünglichen Sujet ermessen. Ein Journalist, der in der *Times* über eine Ausstellung Wains berichtete, schrieb «es ist nicht einmal so, dass er die Katze mit menschlichen Eigenschaften ausstattete, sondern eher, weil er zeigt, wie Katzen sich in menschlichen Situationen verhalten würden; und er tut dies mit einem so einfühlenden Verstehen der viel Katze und mit so Takt und mit einem derart sparsamen Umgang mit den Mitteln, dass wir ihm glauben».

Mehr als dreißig Jahre lang, von den späten Jahren des neunzehnten bis ins frühe zwanzigste Jahrhundert, setzte sich die «Louis-Wain-Katze» als eine vertraute Untergattung der *felis domesticus* durch, unterhielt gleichermaßen Jung und Alt und veränderte

représentait ses sujets en chats, ce qui n'empêchait pas les hommes politiques de l'époque, dont le jeune Winston Churchill, d'être facilement reconnaissable. Wain a toujours démenti avoir caricaturé les chats eux-mêmes. Il apportait néanmoins à ses représentations le même sens aigu de l'observation, la même capacité de réduire ses sujets à quelques détails stylisés en un rapide coup de crayon ou de plume, qui rendent une bonne caricature presque plus vraisemblable qu'un portrait.

A certains égards, le chat Louis Wain semble, en effet, plus félin qu'un vrai chat. Le dessinateur le réduit à ses caractéristiques fondamentales : un museau large et bien en chair sur lequel se dessine une bouche en forme de « V », des yeux énormes, un corps souple comme une poupée de chiffon et de petites pattes rondes visiblement incapables de tenir quoi que ce soit. S'ajoutent à ces traits félins d'autres éléments qui font immédiatement reconnaître le « chat Louis Wain » : son expression humaine, ses habits et ses gestes. Le chat garde son identité féline au moment même où il apparaît le plus humain, signe évident de la maîtrise totale qu'avait Wain de son sujet. A propos d'une de ses expositions, un critique écrivait dans le *Times* : « Ce n'est pas tant parce qu'il investit le chat de caractéristiques humaines, mais parce qu'il montre comment se comporteraient les chats dans des situations humaines – le tout avec une intelligence sympathique de l'être même du chat, du tact et une économie de moyens – que nous le croyons. »

Pendant plus de trente ans, entre la fin du XIXe et le début du XXe siècle, à la plus grande joie d'une foule d'enfants et d'adultes, le chat de Louis Wain s'imposa en tant que sous-famille de *felis domesticus*, tout en faisant subtilement changer les comportements vis-à-vis de son aïeul, le chat domestique lui-même.

the English-speaking world. Yet Wain's personal life was strange and sad, and even his professional life, despite his period of fame, was marred by perpetual financial worries, disappointment and ultimate failure. Like the sad-faced clown, he gave enormous pleasure to others while seeming to have no share reserved for himself.

Louis William Wain was born on 5 August 1860 in Clerkenwell in London.

He was the first of six children, to be followed by five daughters, of whom at least two were also competent artists. None of them married. The youngest suffered from severe mental problems, and when she was thirty she was certified insane and admitted to an asylum. The other four, along with their mother, remained together until their respective deaths, and except for a brief period of independence when he was in his twenties, Louis too shared this somewhat eccentric and reclusive household for most of his life.

After a rather spasmodic schooling – he later admitted to having spent much of his childhood wandering round London while playing truant from school – Louis Wain studied at the West London School of Art, where he afterwards stayed on for a short time as a teacher. When he was only twenty, his father died and Louis became responsible for supporting his mother and five sisters, a burden which he was to carry for the rest of his working life. At the time, however, the burden does not seem to have weighed too heavily, for he soon gave up his teaching job and the only financial security that he was ever to know, in order to concentrate on becoming a free-lance artist.

He was a skilful draughtsman and could turn his hand to many different subjects, but he soon began to specialise in drawing animals and countryside scenes. He worked for a number of different journals including the *Illustrated*

auf subtile Weise die Einstellung zu ihrem Vorfahr im wirklichen Leben, der Hauskatze. Die Zuneigung, die ihr entgegengebracht wurde, wirkte sich auf lange Zeit positiv auf den Respekt gegenüber den Tieren aus, insbesondere auf Katzen. Sie brachte und bringt auch heute noch tausenden von Menschen Vergnügen und Freude. Der Name ihres geistigen Schöpfers wurde zu einem in jedem Haus geläufigen Wort; er wurde in der gesamten englisch sprachigen Welt geschätzt und geliebt. Jedoch war Wains persönliches Leben seltsam und traurig, und selbst sein Berufsleben, auch während der Zeit als er berühmt war, war gezeichnet von fortwährenden finanziellen Sorgen, Enttäuschungen und schließlich seinem Scheitern. Wie der Clown mit dem traurigen Gesicht, spendete er anderen viel Freude, während für ihn selbst davon nichts übrig zu bleiben schien.

Er war das erste von sechs Kindern, ihm folgten fünf Mädchen, von denen mindestens zwei ebenfalls begabte Künstler waren. Keine von ihnen heiratete. Die Jüngste war geistig schwer behindert, mit dreißig wurde sie als geisteskrank eingestuft und in eine Anstalt eingewiesen. Die anderen vier blieben bis an ihr Lebensende mit ihrer Mutter zusammen, und mit Ausnahme eines kurzen Abschnitts, als er in seinen Zwanzigern selbstständig lebte, teilte auch Louis die meiste Zeit das Leben in diesem etwas exzentrischen und einsiedlerischen Haus. Nach einer nur sporadisch absolvierten Schulzeit - er gab später zu, dass er in seiner Jugend, die Schule schwänzend, viel in London unterwegs war - studierte Louis Wain an der *West London School of Art*, wo er danach kurzzeitig auch als Lehrer tätig war. Als Louis erst zwanzig Jahre alt war, starb sein Vater, und er war nun verantwortlich für das Auskommen seiner Mutter und seiner fünf Schwestern; eine Last, die er den Rest seines Arbeitsleben zu tragen haben sollte. Zu diesem Zeitpunkt schien diese Bürde aber nicht allzu schwer auf ihm zu lasten, denn er sollte bald seine Lehrtätigkeit und damit den einzigen Moment finanzieller Sicherheit, den er in sei-

L'affection qu'il inspirait développa durablement le bien-être des animaux en général et celui des chats en particulier. Il a amusé et ravi des dizaines de milliers de personnes, hier comme aujourd'hui. Le nom de Wain devint célèbre, reconnu et aimé à travers le monde anglophone. Sa vie privée fut cependant bizarre et triste ; malgré une période de grande célébrité, de perpétuels soucis d'argent, des déceptions et, finalement, l'échec gâchèrent sa vie professionnelle. Comme le clown triste, il donnait énormément de plaisir aux autres, sans savoir garder, semble-t-il, une parcelle de cette joie pour lui-même.

Louis William Wain naquit le 5 août 1860 à Clerkenwell, à Londres. Aîné de la famille, il était suivi par cinq filles, dont deux au moins furent aussi des artistes authentiques. Aucune ne se maria. Souffrant de graves troubles mentaux, la cadette fut enfermée dans un asile d'aliénés à l'âge de trente ans. Les quatre autres filles et leur mère vécurent ensemble jusqu'à leur mort. Hormis un bref intermède d'indépendance entre vingt et trente ans, Louis aussi partagea cette étrange existence loin du monde.

A l'issue d'une scolarité peu suivie – il reconnut plus tard avoir passé une bonne partie de son enfance à faire l'école buissonnière et à errer dans Londres – Louis Wain étudia à la West London School of Art avant d'y travailler pendant quelque temps comme professeur. A la mort de son père, quand il n'avait que vingt ans, Louis assuma la responsabilité matérielle de sa mère et de ses cinq sœurs, fardeau qu'il devait porter tout le reste de sa carrière. Sans doute insouciant de ses responsabilités, il abandonna son poste de professeur et la seule sécurité financière qu'il devait connaître sa vie durant, pour devenir artiste indépendant.

Dessinateur habile capable de traiter des sujets très différents, Wain se spécialisa rapide-

Sporting and Dramatic News, and the *Illustrated London News*. His black and white work during the 1880s includes some finely detailed 'portraits' of English country houses and their estates, and he was commissioned to travel round the country to visit agricultural shows and make drawings of the livestock there. Dogs, poultry, guinea pigs, fish, pigeons, and many other creatures entered his repertoire at this time, and throughout his life he always retained a facility for drawing animals of all kinds. At one time he hoped to earn a living by making portraits of dogs for their owners. Chance, however, intervened to change his whole career, and coincidentally to revolutionise the status of the cat as a domestic animal in England.

At the age of twenty three Wain, like his father before him, became estranged from his family, though not permanently so. He had married his sisters' governess Emily Richardson, who was ten years older than himself, and set up house with her in Hampstead in north London. Their happiness was short-lived, as she was soon known to be suffering from cancer and died just three years after the marriage, but it was in this period that Wain found his true vocation. During her illness Emily was comforted by the companionship of their pet cat Peter, and Wain taught him tricks to amuse her, such as wearing spectacles and pretending to read a post card, while he filled many sketchbooks with drawings of the cat. 'To him [Peter] properly belongs the foundation of my career, the development of my initial efforts, and the establishing of my work', he was later to write. Peter was a handsome black and white cat, and can be recognised in many of Wain's early published drawings. He also featured in at least one book entirely to himself, and lived on into a respected old age.

In 1886 Wain produced his first humorous picture of anthropomorphic cats, 'A Kittens'

nem Leben gekannt hat, aufgeben, um sich auf sein freischaffendes Künstlerdasein zu konzentrieren.

Er war ein begabter Zeichner und beherrschte viele Sujets, jedoch begann er früh, sich auf das Zeichnen von Tieren und Landschaftsszenen zu spezialisieren. Er arbeitete für eine Reihe verschiedener Zeitschriften, darunter die *Illustrated Sporting and Dramatic News* und die *Illustrated London News*. Unter seinen zwischen 1880 und 1890 entstandenen Schwarzweißwerken waren auch einige sehr detaillierte 'Porträts' englischer Landhäuser mit ihren Anwesen, und er wurde beauftragt, im Land umherzureisen, um Landwirtschaftsschauen zu besuchen und dort das Vieh zu zeichnen. Hunde, Geflügel, Meerschweinchen, Fische, Tauben und viele andere Kreaturen vervollständigten damals sein Repertoire, und sein ganzes Leben lang sollte es ihm besonders leicht fallen, alle Arten von Tieren abzubilden. Eine Zeit lang hoffte er, sein Geld mit dem Zeichnen von Hundeporträts für deren Besitzer verdienen zu können. Der Zufall wollte es jedoch, dass er seine Karriere ändern und gleichzeitig den Status der Katze als Haustier in England revolutionieren sollte.

Im Alter von dreiundzwanzig Jahren nahm er, wie zuvor sein Vater, Abstand er sich von seiner Familie - wenn auch nicht für immer. Er hatte die zehn Jahre ältere Emily Richardson, die Gouvernante seiner Schwestern, geheiratet und ließ sich mit ihr in Hampstead im Norden Londons nieder. Ihr Glück währte aber nur kurz, denn bald stellte man fest, dass Emily an Krebs litt, und sie sollte nur drei Jahre nach ihrer Hochzeit sterben. Es war aber gerade in dieser Zeit, dass Wain seine wahre Berufung entdeckte. Während Emilys Krankheit milderte ihre Katze Peter ihr Leiden. Um Emily aufzuheitern, brachte Wain ihm Kunststückchen bei. So konnte Peter dann eine Brille tragen und so tun, als ob er eine Postkarte lese. Währenddessen füllte Wain manches Skizzenbuch mit Zeichnungen der Katze. Später schrieb er «Ihm [Peter] ist der Beginn meiner Karriere zuzuschreiben, die Fortentwicklung meiner anfänglichen Bemühungen und der Durchbruch meiner Arbeit». Peter

ment dans le dessin d'animaux et de paysages ruraux. Il travailla pour plusieurs publications, dont l'*Illustrated Sporting and Dramatic News* et l'*Illustrated London News*. Dans sa production des années 1880 en noir et blanc, on trouve quelques études très détaillées de grandes demeures anglaises et de leurs terres. On l'envoya dans des foires agricoles à travers le pays pour y dessiner les animaux de ferme. Son répertoire s'élargit pour inclure, entre autres, chiens, volaille, cochons d'Inde, poissons, pigeons. Toute sa vie durant, Wain dessina avec facilité des animaux de toutes sortes. Il espéra un moment gagner sa vie en peignant des chiens pour leurs propriétaires. Le hasard, cependant, transforma toute sa carrière et avec elle bouleversa la place du chat comme animal de compagnie en Angleterre.

Comme son père avant lui, Wain à l'âge de 23 ans quitta sa famille, mais de façon temporaire, en épousant la gouvernante de ses sœurs, une certaine Emily Richardson, de dix ans son aînée. Le couple s'établit à Hampstead, un quartier du nord de Londres, où leur bonheur fut de courte durée. Atteinte d'un cancer, sa femme mourut trois ans seulement après leur mariage. Ce fut pendant sa maladie que Wain découvrit sa véritable vocation. Emily ayant trouvé un certain réconfort dans la compagnie de Peter, le chat de la maison, Wain apprit à celui-ci à jouer des tours pour divertir sa femme. Il lui faisait porter des lunettes et faire semblant de lire une carte postale, pendant qu'il remplissait des carnets entiers de croquis avec des dessins du chat. Wain écrivit plus tard : « C'est grâce à lui (Peter) que j'ai pu fonder ma carrière, développer mes premiers essais et affirmer mon travail. » On reconnaît Peter, un beau chat noir et blanc, dans de nombreux dessins parmi les premiers publiés par Wain. Sujet principal d'un livre qui lui est entièrement consacré, Peter vécut jusqu'à un âge très respectable.

En 1886, pour l'*Illustrated London News*,

Christmas Party', for the Christmas issue of the *Illustrated London News*. It was an instant success, and according to Wain himself, his work was in demand 'from all parts of the world' from that time on. The picture contained 150 cats, several of them clearly identifiable as Peter, and many more which must have been modelled on him. Consisting of a narrative in eleven scenes, it shows the kittens sending out invitations, holding a ball, playing party games, making speeches, and engaging in many of the human activities for which Wain's cats later became renowned. But although the facial expressions of these cats are already beginning to develop some human characteristics, they are little more than the passing resemblance to a human expression which can sometimes be recognised in the features of a real cat. The animals themselves are unclothed and remain firmly on all fours, and even when seated at a table their actions rarely go beyond those of a real cat (such as Peter) performing tricks. The 'Louis Wain cat' had been born, but it had not yet fully developed.

Within a few years, however, it had learnt to walk on its hind legs, had acquired a smile, the triangular eyes which are its hall-mark, and a full range of exaggerated expressions, and was wearing an increasingly elaborate wardrobe of contemporary clothes. It had also learnt to play a variety of musical instruments, and to hold anything from a cup and saucer to a champagne bottle, to a fishing rod, to a meat cleaver, in its rather clumsy front paws. It could ride a bicycle, play golf and cricket, fly aeroplanes, dig holes in the road, flirt, get drunk, and bore its companions with tedious after-dinner speeches. Anything that could with reasonable propriety be done by a human being in public, could be and was done by the Louis Wain cat. Though often engaged in adult activities, however, it re-

war eine schöne Katze mit schwarzweißem Fell, und man findet ihn auf vielen von Wains früh veröffentlichten Zeichnungen wieder. Er spielte auch in mindestens einem Buch die alleinige Hauptrolle und erlangte ein respektables Alter.

Im Jahre 1886 entstand für die Weihnachtsausgabe der *Illustrated London News* «A Kitten's Party», das erste humoristische Bild mit anthropomorphen Katzen. Es war prompt ein Erfolg, und nach Wains Worten wurde sein Werk von diesem Zeitpunkt an «überall auf der Welt» verlangt. Auf dem Bild waren 150 Katzen zu sehen, einige von ihnen waren eindeutig als Peter auszumachen, und auch viele der andern müssen nach seinem Modell entstanden sein. Es handelt sich um eine Erzählung in elf Szenen, die beschreibt, wie die Kätzchen Einladungen verschicken, einen Ball geben, sich bei Partyspielen vergnügen, Reden halten, und sich in manchen eben der menschlichen Aktivitäten ergehen, für die Wains Katzen später bekannt werden sollten. Aber obwohl der Gesichtsausdruck dieser Katzen bereits hier einige menschliche Züge entwickelt, hat er doch wenig mehr als flüchtige Ähnlichkeit mit dem Gesichtsausdruck eines Menschen. Die Tiere selbst sind unbekleidet und bleiben fest auf allen vieren, und selbst wenn sie am Tisch sitzen, geht das, was sie tun, selten über das hinaus, was eine Kunststücke aufführende Katze (wie Peter) auch tun würde. Die «Louis-Wain-Katze» war geboren, aber sie war noch nicht voll entwickelt.

Innerhalb weniger Jahre lernte sie aber, auf ihren Hinterbeinen zu laufen, bekam ein Lächeln, die dreieckigen Augen - ihr Markenzeichen - und eine ganze Reihe übertriebener Züge. Dazu hatte sie einen immer besseren Fundus zeitgenössischer Kleidung. Sie hatte auch gelernt, verschiedene Musikinstrumente zu spielen und mit ihren ziemlich ungelenken Vorderpfoten alles Mögliche zu halten, angefangen von der Tasse samt Unterteller, über die Champagnerflasche bis hin zur Angelrute und dem Fleischermesser. Sie konnte Rad fahren, Golf und Cricket spielen, Flugzeuge fliegen, Löcher in die Straße graben, flirten, sich

Wain exécuta « A Kittens' Christmas Party » (« La fête de Noël des chatons »), sa première représentation humoristique et anthropomorphe de chats. Le succès fut immédiat et à partir de ce moment-là, selon Wain, des demandes d'illustration affluèrent du monde entier. 150 chats y figurent, plusieurs d'entre eux étant de toute évidence des portraits de Peter, tandis que d'autres lui ressemblent. Divisée en onze scènes, l'illustration montre les chatons en train d'envoyer des invitations, d'organiser un bal, de participer à des jeux de société, de prononcer des discours et de s'adonner à toutes ces activités humaines, qui devaient rendre plus tard les chats de Wain si célèbres. Même si les expressions du visage comportent déjà quelques caractéristiques humaines, ce n'est alors guère plus que la ressemblance passagère avec une expression humaine, que l'on devine parfois dans les traits d'un vrai chat. Les animaux ne portent pas de vêtements et restent à quatre pattes. Même lorsque Wain les fait s'asseoir à table, leurs gestes dépassent rarement ceux d'un vrai chat, comme Peter, en train de jouer des tours. Le « chat Louis Wain » était né. Il devait encore beaucoup évoluer.

Quelques années plus tard, le chat avait appris à marcher sur ses pattes de derrière et à sourire. Il avait maintenant les yeux triangulaires, son principal signe distinctif, une variété d'expressions exagérées, et portait une garde-robe de vêtements modernes de plus en plus soignée. Ce chat avait également appris à jouer d'une grand nombre d'instruments de musique et à tenir maladroitement, dans ses pattes de devant, des objets aussi divers qu'une tasse et une soucoupe, une bouteille de champagne, une canne à pêche ou un couteau à viande. Il savait monter à bicyclette, jouer au golf et au cricket, piloter un avion, creuser des trous dans la chaussée, flirter, s'enivrer et ennuyer ses compagnons avec d'as-

mained a mischievous kitten at heart, with a fondness for teasing dogs and creating mayhem in the home and garden.

Anyone who has observed the sleep-to-waking ratio of the average domestic cat will recognise, of course, that the energy level of the Louis Wain cat is actually closer to that of the dog; and there are other doggish elements in its character and behaviour too. But there is also much that is childlike, in its cheerful exuberance, its playfulness, its carefree spirit of adventure, and its determined irresponsibility; and at a time when increasingly sentimental pictures of children featured widely in popular art, the refreshingly anarchic spirit of the Louis Wain child-cat must have helped in fostering its popularity. It certainly has none of the tranquillity, grace, self-sufficiency, aloofness, mystery, or even the cosy fireside companionship, for which many people admire the real-life cat: but although it was aimed primarily at a children's audience, there is no doubt that their parents were charmed by it too.

Wain's cats rapidly established themselves as a part of English life, and for nearly thirty years he continued to turn out a constant stream of original and inventive work. He drew very quickly, and at his peak he was producing several hundred drawings a year. Altogether he illustrated about a hundred children's books, no less than eleven appearing in 1903 alone. His work also appeared in papers, journals and magazines of all kinds, and as numerous post cards and private commissions. From 1901 to 1915, *Louis Wain's Annual* also provided an outlet each year for many more drawings, and his continuing versatility as an illustrator is shown here in various little sketches which he produced as headers or footers for articles by other contributors.

It was in the later editions of the *Annual* too that some of his most sophisticated cartoons

betrinken und nach dem Dinner ihre Begleiter mit öden Reden langweilen. Alles, was von einem menschlichen Wesen mit angemessenem Anstand in der Öffentlichkeit gemacht werden konnte, war erlaubt und wurde von der «Louis-Wain-Katze» gemacht. Wenn sie auch oft mit Erwachsenenangelenheiten befasst war, so blieb sie doch in ihrem Herzen ein schelmisches Kätzchen mit einer Vorliebe dafür, Hunde zu ärgern und im Garten Chaos zu stiften.

Natürlich merkt jeder, der das zwischen Schlafen und Wachen schwankende Dasein der durchschnittlichen Hauskatze studiert hat, dass die Energie der «Louis-Wain-Katze» eigentlich eher der eines Hundes gleichkommt; und es gibt da noch andere hündische Elemente, sowohl in ihrem Charakter als auch in ihrem Benehmen. Indes findet man hier auch vieles, das in seinem fröhlichen Überschwang, seiner Verspieltheit, seinem sorglosen Abenteuergeist und seiner entschiedenen Verantwortungslosigkeit eher etwas von einem Kind hat. Und in einer Zeit, in der die Populärkunst zunehmend von sentimentalen Kinderbildern bestimmt wurde, muss der erfrischend anarchische Geist der kindlichen «Louis-Wain-Katze» dazu beigetragen haben, ihre Popularität zu fördern. Sie hat mit Sicherheit nichts von der Ruhe, der Anmut, der Selbstständigkeit, der Zurückhaltung, des Geheimnisvollen oder sogar dem behaglichen Kumpan am Kamin, weswegen viele Menschen die echte Katze so lieben. Jedoch besteht kein Zweifel, dass auch die Eltern ihrem Charme erlagen. Wains Katzen wurden schnell Teil des englischen Lebens. Und von da an produzierte Wain beinahe dreißig Jahre lang beständig originelle und kreative Arbeiten. Er zeichnete sehr schnell, und am Höhepunkt seines Schaffens produzierte er mehrere hundert Zeichnungen pro Jahr. Insgesamt illustrierte er etwa einhundert Kinderbücher, drei davon erschienen allein im Jahre 1903. Seine Werke wurden in Zeitungen, Journalen und Zeitschriften aller Art gedruckt, dazu zahlreiche als Postkarten und in Privatauftrag. Von 1901 bis 1915 war alljährlich auch

sommants discours après le dîner. Le chat Louis Wain savait accomplir tous les gestes de l'être humain en public, avec élégance. Tout en s'adonnant ordinairement à des activités de grande personne, il restait néanmoins, au fond de lui-même, un chaton espiègle, prenant un malin plaisir à tourmenter les chiens et à semer le désordre à la maison et dans le jardin.

Quiconque a remarqué tout le temps qu'un chat domestique moyen consacre au sommeil reconnaîtra dans le chat Louis Wain un niveau d'énergie bien plus proche de celle du chien. Ce n'est d'ailleurs pas le seul élément du chien qui caractérise sa personnalité et son comportement. De même, on discerne un aspect enfantin dans sa joyeuse exubérance, sa gaieté, son esprit insouciant d'aventure, son étourderie. A une époque où des images d'enfants très sentimentales proliféraient dans l'art populaire, l'esprit du chat-enfant Louis Wain, si frais avec son aspect un peu fou, a dû contribuer à sa popularité. Il ne possède certainement pas le calme, ni l'élégance, l'indépendance, la réserve, le mystère ni même les qualités de compagnon pour lesquelles le vrai chat suscite notre admiration. Destiné principalement à des enfants, le chat Wain devait cependant charmer tout autant leurs parents.

Les chats de Wain s'imposèrent rapidement dans la société anglaise et pendant presque trente ans leur auteur continua à produire un flot d'œuvres inventives et novatrices. Rapide à exécuter ses dessins, il en faisait, au faîte de sa carrière, plusieurs centaines par an. Wain illustra en tout une centaine de livres pour enfants, dont onze parurent pendant la seule année 1903. Il publiait également dans toutes sortes de journaux et de périodiques, illustrait de nombreuses cartes postales et répondait à des commandes privées. Wain fournit de nombreux dessins chaque année de 1901 à 1915 au *Louis Wain's Annual*, tandis

appeared. He had a keen eye for the ridiculous in human behaviour, and would probably be better recognised today as a cartoonist if popular demand had not required all his subjects to be represented as cats. His satire, always mild and generally benign, was directed at humans not at cats, and was at its sharpest when he was gently poking fun at passing fashions of the day. (Perhaps this was a tribute to his notably *un*fashionable mother and sisters, with whom he had returned to live in 1894.) He was thoroughly professional in his working methods, and always continued to draw from the life whenever he could, but this did not mean only from cat life. It was one highly idiosyncratic method of drawing from the life which enabled him to achieve his best results, as he himself explained: 'There is another way of sketching cats, and this way I often resort to. I take a sketch-book to a restaurant, or other public place, and draw the people in their different positions *as cats*, getting as near to their human characteristics as possible. This gives me *doubly* nature, and these studies I think [to be] my best humorous work.'

Wain's lifelong love of animals led inevitably to his becoming involved with all the leading animal welfare charities, especially of course those which were associated with cats. He was a member of the Governing Council of Our Dumb Friends' League, and of the committee for its receiving shelters for stray cats. He was also on the committee for the Society for the Protection of Cats, and was an honorary member of the Anti-Vivisection Society. For many years he was active in running the National Cat Club, both as President and Chairman of the Committee. There was some justification in his claim to have helped 'to wipe out the contempt in which the cat has been held in this country', and to have raised its status 'from the questio-

das *Louis Wain's Annual* ein Ort, wo viele seiner Zeichnungen veröffentlicht wurden. In verschiedenen kleinen Skizzen, die, darunter oder darüber gestellt, die Beiträge anderer illustrierten, zeigt sich auch hier seine andauernde Vielseitigket als Illustrator.

In den späteren Ausgaben des *Annual* erschienen auch einige seiner anspruchsvollsten Cartoons. Er hatte ein scharfes Auge für das Lächerliche im menschlichen Verhalten und wäre heute vielleicht eher als Cartoonist anerkannt, wenn die Menschen damals nicht verlangt hätten, dass all seine Sujets als Katzen darzustellen seien. Seine Satire, die stets sachte und im Allgemeinen gutmütig war, richtete sich an die Menschen, nicht an die Katzen, und erreichte ihren Höhepunkt wenn er sich leise über die vergänglichen Moden der damaligen Zeit lustig machte. (Vielleicht war dies ein Tribut an seine bemerkenswert *un*moderne Mutter und seine ebenso *un*modernen Schwestern, zu denen er 1894 zurückkehrte.) In seinen Arbeitsmethoden war er durch und durch professionell und er zeichnete weiterhin, wann immer es ihm möglich war, aus dem Leben. Das heißt aber nicht, dass er ausschließlich aus dem Leben der Katzen zeichnete. Wie er selbst erklärte, erlaubte es ihm eine sehr eigenwillige Methode, aus dem Leben zu zeichnen, seine besten Ergebnisse zu erzielen: «Es gibt eine andere Art, Katzen zu skizzieren, und dieser Methode bediene ich mich oft. Ich nehme ein Skizzenbuch mit in ein Restaurant oder an einen anderen öffentlichen Ort und zeichne die Menschen in ihren verschiedenen Positionen *als Katzen* und komme so ihren menschlichen Eigenschaften so nahe wie nur möglich. Damit erfasse ich das Wesen *zweifach*, und ich denke, diese Studien sind meine besten humoristischen Arbeiten.»

Wains Liebe zu Tieren, die sein ganzes Leben lang andauerte, führte unvermeidbar dazu, dass er sich am Wirken aller führenden Organisationen beteiligte, die sich um das Wohl von Tieren kümmerten, insbesondere natürlich solcher, die etwas mit Katzen zu tun hatten. Er war Mitglied im Governing Council of Our Dumb Friend's League und auch in dessen Ko-

que diverses petites esquisses destinées à accompagner, en haut ou en bas de page, les articles d'autres collaborateurs, témoignent de sa très grande souplesse en tant qu'illustrateur.

Quelques-uns de ses dessins les plus élaborés parurent dans les dernières éditions de l'*Annual*. Observateur aigu de tous les ridicules du comportement humain, Wain serait aujourd'hui mieux reconnu en tant que caricaturiste si la demande populaire n'avait exigé que ses sujets apparaissent sous la forme de chats. C'est lorsqu'il taquinait les modes éphémères de l'époque que son sens de l'ironie dirigé contre les humains et non contre les chats, léger et généralement sans méchanceté, était le plus mordant (on peut y voir, peut-être, un hommage à sa mère et ses sœurs, très « vieux jeu », auprès desquelles il était retourné vivre en 1894). Très professionnel dans ses méthodes de travail, Wain continua toujours à dessiner aussi souvent que possible sur le vif. Ce qui ne signifiait pas pour autant dessiner seulement des chats. Il parvint à ses résultats les plus convaincants grâce à une méthode de dessin sur le vif éminemment personnelle. Il l'expliqua lui-même : « Il existe une autre façon d'esquisser des chats à laquelle j'ai souvent recours. J'apporte un carnet au restaurant, ou dans un autre endroit public, et je dessine les gens dans leurs diverses postures comme des chats, en me rapprochant le plus près possible de leurs caractéristiques humaines. La nature est ainsi rendue doublement, et je considère que ces croquis sont mon meilleur travail humoristique. »

L'amour de Wain pour les animaux, qui dura toute sa vie, l'amena inévitablement à s'engager auprès des plus importantes associations de protection des animaux et en premier lieu de celles qui s'occupaient de chats. Il fut membre du conseil d'administration de Our Dumb Friends' League ainsi que du comité chargé des

nable care and affection of the old maid to a real and permanent place in the home', though he was only part of a movement which was already under way by the time he embarked on his career. The first English cat show took place at the Crystal Palace in 1871, indicating a rising interest in the cat as something more than a mere animated mouse-trap. But cat breeding and cat shows have a limited audience, even today, and in truth the Louis Wain cat, through its sheer numbers and its power to infiltrate to the very heart of the family, probably made a stronger impact on the general public.

Despite his fame, popularity and apparent success Wain never became rich, and never even earned enough money to be comfortable. He was the sole bread-winner in a family of six, though his mother and unfashionable sisters were far from extravagant, living quietly and often dressing in second-hand clothes. As a free-lance artist he had to work immensely hard, not only at making but selling his drawings, and he was certainly no businessman. A modest, diffident, self-effacing man, impractical in the affairs of everyday life, he was ill-equipped to deal with the shark-infested waters of journalistic publishing. He disliked bargaining and was easily exploited, and generally sold his work outright so that he earned nothing from subsequent reproduction fees. He lived perpetually on the brink, and would sometime have to borrow his train fare home after selling a drawing, if he was paid by cheque. During the worst period, when he was unable to pay his household bills, the 'Louis Wain cat' itself became an item of currency. Sometimes he would settle an account by making a hasty sketch on the spot: at the least, such a drawing could appease and fend off the debt-collector, for Wain himself was well liked, and those who knew his situation were always sympathetic and willing to help.

mitee, das sich um ein Heim für streunende Katzen kümmerte. Ebenfalls war er im Komitee der Society for the Protection of Cats und Ehrenmitglied der Anti-Vivisection Society. Viele Jahre lang war er aktiv im National Cat Club tätig, sowohl als dessen Präsident als auch als Komitee-Vorsitzender. Es ist etwas Wahres daran, wenn er für sich in Anspruch nimmt, «die Verachtung, die der Katze in diesem Land entgegengebracht wurde, ausgelöscht zu haben» und ihren Status «von einer fragwürdigen Sorge und Zuneigung dem 'alten Mädchen' gegenüber zu einem realen und dauerhaften Platz daheim» aufgewertet zu haben. Allerdings war er nur Teil der Bewegung, die schon aktiv war, als er sich ihr anschloss. Im Jahre 1871 fand im Crystal Palace dann auch die erste Katzenausstellung statt und machte ein steigendes Interesse an der Katze als etwas mehr als einer lebenden Mausefalle deutlich. Indes sprachen, damals wie heute, die Katzenzucht und Katzenausstellungen nur ein beschränktes Publikum an, und in Wahrheit hatte womöglich die «Louis-Wain-Katze» durch ihre enorme Präsenz und ihre Fähigkeit, in das Herz jeder Familie vorzudringen, einen größeren Einfluss auf die Öffentlichkeit als die echte Katze.

Trotz seines Ruhms, seiner Beliebtheit und seines offensichtlichen Erfolges wurde Wain nie reich, ja er verdiente nicht einmal genug, um ein vernünftiges Leben führen zu können. Er war der einzige Brotverdiener in einer fünfköpfigen Familie. Und auch die Tatsache, dass seine Mutter und seine Schwestern sich nicht den Moden unterwarfen und alles andere als extravagant waren, änderte nichts an Wains finanziellen Sorgen. Als freischaffender Künstler musste er nicht nur beim Schaffen seiner Werke, sondern auch für deren Verkauf enorm hart arbeiten. Dazu kam, dass er alles andere als ein Geschäftsmann war. Als bescheidener, schüchterner und zurückhaltender Mensch, ungeschickt in Fragen des täglichen Lebens, war er schlecht gerüstet, um in den haifischverseuchten Gewässern des journalistischen Verlagswesens zu bestehen. Er hatte eine Abneigung gegen Verhandlungen

abris pour chats perdus. Il fit également partie du comité de la Society for the Protection of Cats, tout en étant membre honoraire de l'Anti-Vivisection Society. Pendant de nombreuses années, il joua un rôle actif dans les instances dirigeantes du National Cat Club, tant comme président que comme directeur de son comité.

Sa revendication de devoir « effacer le mépris avec lequel on a considéré le chat dans ce pays » et de l'avoir fait grimper « de la protection et de l'affection discutables de la vieille fille à une place authentique et durable à la maison » est en partie justifiée. Mais, en fait, il n'était qu'un élément d'un mouvement déjà lancé au moment où il commença sa carrière. Le premier « English cat show », exposition consacrée aux chats, avait eu lieu au Crystal Palace de Londres en 1871, signe d'un intérêt grandissant pour un animal considéré comme autre chose qu'un simple piège à souris sur quatre pattes. Mais, même aujourd'hui, l'élevage et les expositions de chats attirent un public relativement limité. Par sa simple prolifération et sa capacité à pénétrer jusqu'au cœur de la famille, le chat Louis Wain frappa probablement beaucoup plus l'esprit du grand public.

Malgré sa notoriété, sa popularité et son succès apparent, Wain ne fut jamais financièrement à l'aise. Il devait subvenir seul aux besoins de sa mère et de ses quatre sœurs, même si celles-ci, peu soucieuses de mode, vivaient très simplement, s'habillant souvent avec des vêtements d'occasion. Artiste indépendant, Wain devait travailler dur, non seulement pour réaliser ses dessins mais également pour les vendre. Il fut tout sauf un bon homme d'affaires. Modeste, timide, peu sûr de lui et manquant de sens pratique, Wain se trouvait désarmé dans la jungle du journalisme. Détestant le marchandage, facile à exploiter, il vendait son travail le plus souvent au forfait, sacrifiant ainsi ses droits

For many years he maintained an ill-founded confidence that some new scheme or invention was just about to make his fortune. Sometimes it was a new project or invention of his own which failed, sometimes he was duped or misled by others. In 1907 he went to America and spent two years there. He did some work for the Hearst Newspapers, and was fêted and admired, interviewed about cats, and invited to judge cat shows all over the country: but he had certainly not made his fortune by the time he returned home (brought back by the news of his mother's death). Worse still, he may even have lost any savings that he had by imprudent investment, in an unsuccessful invention for a new type of lamp.

From this time onwards he had increasing difficulty in obtaining new work. To some extent he was the victim of his own success. Trapped in a fashionable cult whose popularity could not be expected to last forever, he had no escape route when the market began to close down. By the time the First World War broke out he was already in serious financial difficulties, and inevitably the outlets for his work diminished still further. In times of war and paper-shortages, the comic cartoon cat is not a protected species. The Wain family began to fall into real poverty and debt.

Louis Wain's mental decline seems to have begun around this time, though how far it was hastened by the anxiety and struggle to pay his bills, and how far his loosening grip on reality increased his other troubles, is not clear. His gradual deterioration seems to have taken place over a long period. He had always been a strange, shy, 'other-worldly' man, regarded by everyone who knew him as charming but eccentric. His ideas, as well as his mode of expressing them, were often opaque and sometimes almost incomprehensible, and even where his own life

und wurde leicht ausgenommen, zudem verkaufte er seine Arbeiten in der Regel sofort und konnte so nichts an späteren Reproduktionen verdienen. Er lebte ständig am Rande des finanziellen Ruins, und wenn ihm ein Gemälde per Scheck bezahlt wurde, musste er sich zuweilen Geld leihen, um seine Zugfahrkarte nach Hause kaufen zu können. In seiner schlimmsten Zeit, als er nicht in der Lage war, die Haushaltsrechnungen zu bezahlen, wurde die «Louis-Wain-Katze» selbst zum Zahlungsmittel. Manchmal beglich er eine Rechnung, indem er aus dem Stegreif eine Zeichnung anfertigte; zumindest konnte sie den Gläubiger besänftigen und ihn somit vorerst abwehren, denn Wain selbst war sehr beliebt und die, die seine Situation kannten, waren immer mitfühlend und bereit, ihm zu helfen.

Viele Jahre lang hegte er die kaum begründete Hoffnung, dass irgendein neues Konzept oder eine Erfindung ihm demnächst ein Vermögen bescheren würde. Manchmal war es ein eigenes neues Vorhaben oder eine Erfindung, die fehlschlug, manchmal wurde er getäuscht oder von anderen irregeführt. Im Jahre 1907 ging er nach Amerika und verbrachte dort zwei Jahre. Er arbeitete für die *Hearst Newspaper*, wurde gefeiert und bewundert, über Katzen interviewt, zur Beurteilung von Katzenschauen im ganzen Land eingeladen, aber als er (wegen der Nachricht vom Tode seiner Mutter) zurückkehrte, hatte er ganz sicher kein Vermögen verdient. Es war noch schlimmer, denn bei einer unvorsichtigen Investition in eine erfolglose Erfindung, einen neuen Lampentyp, hat er wohl seine gesamten Ersparnisse verloren. Obwohl unklar ist, inwieweit er durch seine finanziellen Sorgen beschleunigt wurde, und obgleich auch nicht geklärt ist, inwiefern sein zunehmender Realitätsverlust seine anderen Probleme verstärkten, scheint Louis Wains geistiger Niedergang in etwa dieser Zeit eingesetzt zu haben. Die sich schrittweise vollziehende Verschlechterung seines Gesundheitszustandes hat sich wohl über einen langen Zeitraum hingezogen. Er war immer ein seltsamer, schüchterner Mann gewesen, der 'aus einer an-

d'auteur. Comme il vivait au jour le jour, il lui fallait parfois emprunter le prix de son billet de train pour retourner chez lui si son client lui payait un dessin par chèque. Dans les moments les plus difficiles, lorsqu'il n'arrivait plus à couvrir les frais de la famille, le « chat Louis Wain » lui-même devenait une monnaie d'échange. Wain réglait parfois une dette en exécutant sur le champ un rapide croquis qui parvenait ainsi à calmer ou à faire patienter un agent de recouvrement. Ceux qui connaissaient la situation de cet artiste très populaire se montraient toujours compréhensifs et prêts à l'aider.

Pendant de longues années, Wain crut naïvement qu'il était sur le point de faire fortune grâce à un projet nouveau ou une idée originale. Mais soit ses propres projets échouaient, soit il était victime de la duperie de son entourage. En 1907, il partit aux Etats-Unis, où il passa deux ans, travaillant notamment pour le groupe de presse *Hearst Newspapers*. Admiré et choyé, interviewé sur les chats, invité dans le jury des expositions de chats partout dans le pays, Wain n'avait cependant pas réussi à faire fortune lorsqu'il dut regagner l'Angleterre à la mort de sa mère. Il semble même qu'il ait alors perdu les faibles économies dont il disposait avec l'échec d'une nouvelle sorte de lampe dans laquelle il avait imprudemment investi. A partir de là, victime jusqu'à un certain point de son propre succès, Wain éprouva de plus en plus de mal à trouver du travail. Pris au piège d'un culte qui ne pouvait s'éterniser, il ne trouva plus de solution de rechange lorsque la demande commença à diminuer. Au début de la Première Guerre mondiale, il était en proie à de graves problèmes financiers. Les débouchés pour son travail devinrent inéluctablement de moins en moins nombreux. En période de guerre et de pénurie de papier, le chat de bande dessinée humoristique n'était guère une espèce protégée. La famille Wain commença à s'enfoncer dans la pauvreté et l'endettement.

was concerned, he had difficulty in distinguishing between fact and fantasy. He claimed, for example, to have educated himself in the physical sciences while playing truant from school, and that he had had to choose between music (for which he did have an undoubted talent), painting, authorship, and chemistry for his career. Throughout his life he referred to the study of science and chemistry as being among his chief interests: but some of the more bizarre pseudo-scientific theories which he recounted to his interviewers suggest that the possible career in chemistry lay firmly in the realm of fantasy. His writings too suggest that he would not have got very far in 'authorship'. Although some did get into print, including several long and rambling letters to newspapers on topics of the day, there is always a feeling about them of being only lightly anchored in reality, as though the subject might at any moment fly off at a tangent and get lost.

One might indeed say of Louis Wain's whole life that it was only lightly anchored in reality, that anchor being his art. It may be no coincidence that his hold on reality began to slip at the same time that his art began to be rejected, but there is no doubt that serious mental disorder was gradually replacing mere eccentricity. His personality and behaviour changed, and he began to suffer from outright delusions. From being a mild-tempered man, full of goodwill towards everyone, and certainly too trusting of other people for his own good, he became obstinate and suspicious. He was hostile towards his remaining sisters, accusing them of robbing him, and holding them responsible for the death of Caroline, the eldest (who had actually died in the influenza epidemic of 1917). He claimed that the flickering of the cinema screen had taken the electricity out of their brains, and wrote abusive letters about them to friends. He

deren Welt' zu kommen schien, und jeder, der ihn kannte, fand ihn charmant, aber exzentrisch. Seine Ideen sowie die Art, wie er sie zum Ausdruck brachte, waren oft undurchsichtig und mitunter praktisch unverständlich. Und selbst wenn sein eigenes Leben betroffen war, tat er sich schwer, Tatsachen von seiner Fanatsie zu unterscheiden. Er behauptete zum Beispiel, dass er sich während des Schulschwänzens in den Naturwissenschaften gebildet habe und dass er sich für seine Karriere zwischen der Musik (für die er unzweifelhaft ein Talent besaß), der Malerei, der Schriftstellerei und der Chemie entscheiden musste. Sein ganzes Leben lang nannte er das Studium der Naturwissenschaften und das der Chemie als seine Interessenschwerpunkte. Einige seiner bizzareren pseudo-wissenschaftlichen Theorien, die er in Interviews verbreitete, lassen jedoch darauf schließen, dass seine mögliche Karriere in der Chemie eindeutig dem Reich der Fantasie entsprang. Auch seine schriftlichen Zeugnisse legen den Schluss nahe, dass er es als Autor nicht weit gebracht hätte. Obwohl einiges sehr wohl gedruckt wurde, einschließlich mehrerer langer, weitschweifiger Briefe an Zeitungen zu Themen der damaligen Zeit, hat man bei ihm immer das Gefühl, dass das, was er schreibt, nur schwach in der Realität verankert ist, so als ob er in jedem Moment vom Thema abkommen und es verlieren könne. Man möchte in der Tat sagen, dass Louis Wains ganzes Leben nur schwach in der Realität verankert war, denn sein Anker war die Kunst. Vielleicht war es kein Zufall, dass ihm der Realitätsbezug in der Zeit zu entgleiten begann, als seine Kunst immer mehr abgelehnt wurde. Indes besteht kein Zweifel, dass schwere geistige Störungen Schritt für Schritt die reine Exzentrik ersetzten. Sowohl seine Persönlichkeit als auch sein Verhalten veränderten sich, und er litt zusehends an reinem Wahn. Einst ein sanftmütiger Mensch, voll guten Willens zu jedermann, der anderen gegenüber freilich zu vertrauensvoll war - und dies ist positiv gemeint -, wurde er eigensinnig und misstrauisch. Im Umgang

La santé mentale de Louis Wain dut commencer à se détériorer à cette époque, même si on peut difficilement savoir à quel point l'angoisse des factures impayées l'accéléra et, inversement, jusqu'où de perdre pied avec la réalité aggrava ses problèmes matériels. La dégradation de sa santé semble s'être étalée sur une longue période. Wain avait toujours été un homme étrange, timide et détaché du monde, perçu par tous ceux qui le fréquentaient comme charmant mais excentrique. Ses idées, souvent aussi obscures que sa façon de les exprimer, étaient parfois quasiment incompréhensibles. Il éprouvait de plus en plus de mal à faire dans sa propre vie la distinction entre l'imagination et la réalité. Il affirmait ainsi avoir appris la physique tout seul, pendant qu'il faisait l'école buissonnière, et avoir été obligé de choisir une carrière entre la musique (pour laquelle il possédait un talent indéniable), la peinture, la littérature ou la chimie. Tout au long de sa vie, Wain aima dire qu'il s'intéressait tout particulièrement à l'étude de la chimie et de la physique. Certaines de ses théories pseudo-scientifiques les plus farfelues laissent cependant supposer qu'une hypothétique carrière dans la chimie aurait relevé de la plus pure fantaisie. Ses écrits incitent à penser qu'une carrière en littérature aurait également fait long feu. Certains, en effet, dont quelques longues lettres décousues, traitant de sujets d'actualité, furent publiés par des journaux auxquels il les avait envoyés. Ils donnent néanmoins l'impression que Wain entretenait un contact superficiel avec la réalité, comme si le sujet risquait à tout moment de s'envoler et de lui échapper.

On pourrait en dire autant de toute la vie de Wain, où l'art constitua un lien fragile avec la réalité. Ce n'est peut-être pas un effet du hasard si ce lien commença justement à se briser au moment même où l'on se mit à rejeter son art. Il est certain, en revanche, que son excentricité céda peu à peu le pas à de graves troubles men-

started to rearrange rooms and move furniture about the house, wandered into the street in the middle of the night leaving the door wide open, and spent a lot of time shut up in his room writing – sometimes semi-coherent ramblings, sometimes strings of meaningless words.

He continued to draw and illustrated several more books, but they were not very successful. His behaviour became more unmanageable and finally his sisters could no longer cope, after he had almost knocked one of them downstairs and pushed another out of the house with his hands round her throat. In 1924 he was certified insane and admitted to a pauper ward of Springfield Mental Hospital, the former Surrey County Asylum. He was 'discovered' here a year later. When the newspapers publicised his fate, people were shocked and saddened. Appeals were set up, the message from H.G.Wells was broadcast, and in 1925, after the personal intervention of the Prime Minister, Wain was transferred to the Bethlem Royal Hospital, then one of the leading psychiatric hospitals in the country. He might have remained comfortably here for the rest of his life, but in 1930 the hospital closed briefly before moving to new premises, and Wain was transferred to Napsbury Hospital near St Albans in Hertfordshire, north of London. This was a relatively new and pleasant mental hospital with beautiful gardens, and a thriving cat colony, where he remained until his death in 1939.

His final fifteen years were comparatively tranquil, once he had settled down to hospital life. His gentle and courteous manner returned, though he became increasingly confused and deluded, and the nurses thought it a privilege to care for so famous a person. Above all, he was still able to draw. Now that he did not have to earn a living, he could indulge his

mit seinen Schwestern wurde er feindselig und bezichtigte sie, ihn zu bestehlen. Außerdem machte er sie für den Tod von Caroline, der Ältesten, verantwortlich, die in Wirklichkeit infolge der Grippe-Epidemie im Jahre 1917 verstorben war. Er behauptete, dass das Flimmern der Kinoleinweind sie der Elektrizität ihrer Gehirne beraubt habe, und er schrieb an Freunde ausfällige Briefe über sie. Er begann, die Räume umzugestalten und Möbel im Haus hin- und herzuräumen, ging mitten in der Nacht auf die Straße und ließ die Tür sperrangelweit offen stehen; er verbrachte viel Zeit eingeschlossen in seinem Zimmer und schriftstellerte - manchmal halbwegs zusammenhängendes, weit ausschweifendes Geschreibsel, manchmal nur Abfolgen sinnloser Wörter.

Weiterhin zeichnete er auch und illustrierte mehrere Bücher, jedoch waren sie nicht sehr erfolgreich. Sein Verhalten wurde immer unberechenbarer und schließlich, nachdem er eine von ihnen beinahe die Treppe hinunter- und eine andere, seine Hände um ihren Hals geklammert, aus dem Haus gestoßen hatte, konnten seine Schwestern nicht länger mit ihm umgehen. Im Jahre 1924 wurde er als geisteskrank eingestuft und in eine Armenstation des Springfield Mental Hospital, dem ehemaligen Surrey County Asylum, eingewiesen. Hier wurde er ein Jahr später «entdeckt». Als die Zeitungen sein Schicksal an die Öffentlichkeit brachten, waren die Menschen geschockt und betrübt. Hilfeappelle wurden aufgesetzt, die Botschaft H.G. Wells' wurde gesendet und 1925, nach persönlicher Intervention des Premierministers, wurde Wain in das Bethlem Royal Hospital verlegt, das damals eines der führenden psychatrischen Kliniken des Landes war. Hier hätte er wohl bequem für den Rest seines Lebens bleiben können, aber 1930, bevor die Klinik in neue Gebäude umziehen sollte, schloss es kurzzeitig, und Wain wurde in das Napsbury Hospital in der Nähe des nördlich von London gelegenen St. Albans in Hertfordshire verlegt. Dies war eine relativ neue und

taux. Sa personnalité et son comportement changèrent et il commença à souffrir d'hallucinations. Cet homme d'un tempérament facile, bienveillant envers tout le monde et sans doute trop confiant en autrui pour ses propres affaires, devint entêté et méfiant. Agressif envers ses sœurs, il les accusa de le voler et tint les trois survivantes pour responsables de la mort de Caroline, la sœur aînée, victime de l'épidémie de grippe de 1917. Convaincu également que la lumière scintillante des écrans de cinéma avait « vidé l'électricité de leurs cerveaux », Wain écrivait des propos injurieux à leur sujet dans des lettres à ses amis. Il se mit à déplacer sans raison le mobilier de leur maison et sortait en plein milieu de la nuit pour errer dans les rues, laissant la porte grande ouverte derrière lui. Le reste du temps, il passait de longues heures enfermé dans sa chambre à écrire tantôt des élucubrations à peine cohérentes, tantôt des suites de mots dénués de sens.

Wain continuait pourtant à dessiner et il illustra encore plusieurs livres, qui n'eurent pas grand succès. Ses sœurs n'étaient plus en mesure de faire face à un comportement de plus en plus incontrôlable : en la bousculant, Wain fit tomber l'une d'elles dans l'escalier et en fit sortir une autre dans la rue, en lui serrant très fort le cou. En 1924, il fut reconnu comme aliéné mental et admis dans la section pour indigents de Springfield Mental Hospital, l'ancien Surrey Country Asylum. C'est là que la presse le « découvrit » un an plus tard, au scandale et à la grande tristesse des lecteurs. On organisa des appels à la générosité du public et H.G. Wells diffusa son message. Après l'intervention du Premier ministre en personne, on transféra Wain en 1925 au Bethlem Royal Hospital, l'un des meilleurs hôpitaux psychiatriques du pays. Wain aurait pu y rester tranquillement jusqu'à la fin de ses jours, si l'hôpital n'avait dû fermer

liking for brightly coloured and fanciful landscapes, flowers, and patterns of all kinds, though cats remained his principal theme. At Napsbury he painted colourful cats as Christmas decorations on the huge mirrors in his ward (two of which are now in the collection of his work in the Bethlem Hospital Museum), and he was generous in drawing cats for staff and visitors alike, many of which were handed down as treasured possessions in the families of those who received them. And whenever a real-life cat or kitten crossed his path, it was rapidly immortalised on paper as a Louis Wain cat.

Life may have failed to reward Louis Wain as he deserved, for the innocent pleasure which he had given to so many people: but the cat did not let him down. As Peter had so long ago comforted his dying wife, and incidentally helped to lay the foundations of his own career, the Louis Wain cat remained with its creator to the end. It now lives on to ensure that he is not forgotten.

Patricia ALLDERIDGE

angenehme Nervenklinik mit wunderschönen Gärten und einer prächtig gedeihenden Katzenkolonie. Dort blieb er bis zu seinem Tode im Jahre 1939.

Nachdem er sich an das Leben im Krankenhaus gewöhnt hatte, waren seine letzten fünfzehn Jahre vergleichsweise ruhig. Obwohl er zunehmend verwirrt war, hatte er seine sanfte und höfliche Art zurückgewonnen, und die Schwestern betrachteten es als Privileg, für einen so berühmten Menschen sorgen zu dürfen. Vor allem konnte er noch immer zeichnen. Und nun, da er sich nicht mehr um seinen Lebensunterhalt kümmern musste, konnte er, obwohl Katzen sein Hauptthema blieben, sich seiner Vorliebe für farbenfrohe, phantasievolle Landschaften, Blumen und Muster hingeben. Als Weihnachtsdekoration zeichnete er in Napsbury auf die riesigen Spiegel seiner Station Katzen in prächtigen Farben (zwei davon befinden sich jetzt in der Sammlung seiner Werke im Bethlem Hospital Museum), und er war auch allgemein sehr großzügig mit dem Zeichnen von Katzen, sowohl für das Personal als auch für Besucher. Viele von ihnen werden in den Familien, die diese Zeichnungen damals erhalten haben, als wertvoller Besitz weitervererbt. Und wann immer eine echte, lebende Katze seinen Weg kreuzte, wurde sie schnell auf Papier gebracht und so als «Louis-Wain-Katze» unsterblich gemacht.

Das Leben mag Louis Wain für die naive Freude, die er vielen Menschen gebracht hat, nicht so belohnt haben, wie er es verdient hätte; die Katze ließ ihn jedoch nicht im Stich. So wie Peter vor langer Zeit seine sterbende Frau getröstet hatte, und nebenbei dazu beigetragen hatte, den Grundstein zu seiner Karriere zu legen, so blieb die «Louis-Wain-Katze» bis zu seinem Ende bei ihm. Sie überlebte ihn und sorgt dafür, dass er nicht vergessen wird.

pour être réaménagé ailleurs. Wain fut transféré à Napsbury Hospital, près de St Albans dans le Hertfordshire, au nord de Londres. Jusqu'à sa mort en 1939, il vécut dans cet hôpital neuf et agréable, entouré de très beaux jardins et d'une joyeuse colonie de chats.

Dès qu'il fut habitué à la vie en hôpital, Wain passa les quinze dernières années de sa vie d'une manière relativement paisible. L'esprit de plus en plus embrouillé, sujet à des hallucinations, il retrouva néanmoins son caractère gentil et courtois d'autrefois : les infirmières, elles, se montraient fières de soigner un personnage aussi célèbre. L'essentiel était que Wain arrivait encore à dessiner. Débarrassé du souci de gagner sa vie, il se laissait aller à un penchant pour des paysages fantaisistes aux couleurs vives, à des fleurs et à des motifs très divers, son thème principal demeurant toutefois les chats. En guise de décoration de Noël, il peignait des chats en couleur sur les énormes glaces qui se trouvaient dans sa salle de l'hôpital à Napsbury : deux d'entre eux figurent aujourd'hui dans la collection des œuvres de Wain au Bethlem Hospital Museum. Il se montrait tout aussi généreux en dessinant des chats pour le personnel de l'hôpital et pour les visiteurs, dont les familles et leurs descendants conservèrent souvent ces croquis précieusement. Chaque fois que l'artiste apercevait un vrai chat ou un chaton, il l'immortalisait rapidement sur papier sous forme d'un chat Louis Wain.

La vie ne récompensa sans doute pas Louis Wain comme il l'aurait mérité, lui qui avait donné du plaisir à tant de gens : mais le chat, lui, ne le trahit pas. Tout comme Peter avait réconforté sa femme mourante et, ce faisant, l'avait aidé à lancer sa carrière, le chat Louis Wain resta avec son créateur jusqu'à la fin. Aujourd'hui, en lui survivant, il le sauve de l'oubli.

Louis Wain.

Louis Wain.

5. Then he discovers that he has attacked the King

and he is put on bread & water for a month.

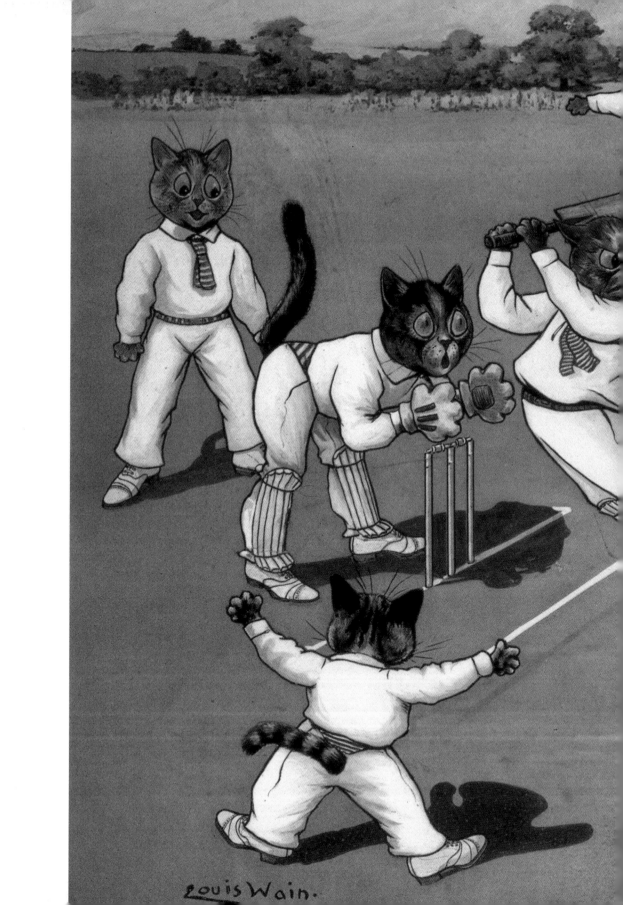

Louis Wain.

Louis Wain.

Louis Wain.

LouisWain.

London, CHRIS BEETLES   17-18-19-20-21-22-23-24-25-27
31-36-38-39-40-41-43-44-48-49
53-54-55-59-62-63-64-69-73-74
75-77-78-79-82-83-84-89-91-92

London, VICTORIA AND ALBERT MUSEUM   28-29-30-32-33-34-35-37-46
50-51-57-65-81-85

Paris, BRIDGEMAN ART LIBRARY   42-45-47-56-60-61-66-67-68
70-71-86-87-88-93-95